IT'S ALL GOOD

KAREN KELLOCK PH.D.

Manual for
Superior Men

A complete theory based on Einstein physics, Political Psychology, Systems Theory and Archetypal Psychiatry.

FORMULA

All success attraction
All disease obstruction
All recovery elimination

You must fast on all three
OBSTRUCTIONS:
People
Habit
Food

IT'S ALL GOOD

The unique can't endure remarks from retards so become increasingly isolated seeming even more bizarre.

A deep empath is tortured by gossip and ridicule and it's the reason genius dies early from drugs and alcohol.

It helped immensely to know it wasn't Tom, Dick or Harry I was mad at but being imposed on by ALL idiots.

IT'S ALL GOOD

DO YOU HAVE THE GUTS TO BE ALONE
ONLY PROBLEM IS WHEN THEY COME AROUND
BAD DEALS
DEPRESSION
DEPRESSION IS A BIT NARCISSISTIC
COMPENSATORY DEVICES
YOU'RE CREATING THE FEELINGS
LETTING GO OF PAST
PRACTICE LETTING IT GO
YOU WENT THRU THAT TO BUILD A BATTLESHIP
SEX AND LIBERALS
REPLACEABILITY BY NARCISSISTS
HE THINKS HE CAN REPLACE YOU?
HANDLING DISRESPECT
RECOGNIZE—OR IT MAGNIFIES
CANNIBUS: AWAY WITH YA'
COUGH TILL IT'S GONE
UNACKNOWLEDGED SIGNS OF DISRESPECT
THE SILENT TREATMENT
A LOVER WON'T PLAY GAMES
SET A BOUNDARY BABY
THE DUKE AND DUCHESS
THE UK IS RACIST MEGHAN SAYS
THE NEW AGE AIN'T SAGACIOUS
HE PUTS YOU THRU THE RINGER
SOCIAL MEDIA AND THE NARCISSIST
NARCISSISTS AND SOCIAL MEDIA
WALK AWAY AND MEAN IT
GREATNESS WALKS AWAY BABY
WORKING ON YOURSELF ALWAYS WORKS
PURSUE WHAT YOU LIKE
LIKE LIKES LIKE
CORONAVIRUS
LIBERAL POOPING IN THE CITY
IT'S ALL BEEN PLANNED
PEOPLE ARE DROPPING DEAD
MARTIAL LAW AND QUARANTINE TRAINING
HIX POLITIX

IT'S ALL GOOD

IT'S ALL GOOD

If you're not playing the leading role it means you're disposable. You're number ONE or just say "no".

DO YOU HAVE THE GUTS TO BE ALONE

Do you have the guts to say I **WANT TO BE ALONE** or do you make excuses? Assert yourself or be abused.

What a revelation to me that I was happy and blissful in my **NATURAL** state-- just me, all alone = first rate.

Next revelation: I did not need **ANYONE** to fulfill me--in fact they always distracted and aggravated me.

We're ever-searching for fulfillment but no human or external object can do that--that's the paradox.

Not just for depressives but everyone: it all comes down to your inner psychology and reactions to situations.

If you're in a bad situation and depressed, how is that clinical or genetic? In psychology it's a mess.

If you're so anxious about rubbing em the wrong way or getting their disapproval that's a bummer Mabel.

Or being so busy living up to how you should look, how many friends you should have--blah blah blah

On a deep level it's really a misunderstanding of what happiness really is. Going **INSIDE = BLISS**.

SOLUTIONS: Firstly, do introspection and see how ego is creating depression. Go deeper for the solution.

IT'S ALL GOOD

Before I found myself I was naturally unhappy adapting to others. Sister said: get on the pills or it's over.

Women on anti-d's are pill-pushers and thus this cultural malady spreads and they're never really better.

When it hits the mark I always think "wow this was so much easier than I thought" and its the goodness of God.

Left-right arguments always turn into yelling matches and are entirely useless. There is disorder, of course.

ONLY PROBLEM IS WHEN THEY COME AROUND

Even though I knew I was moving on up to a higher station I didn't want to leave my little cabin.

My tiny cabin in the desert wilderness with a 1000 acre buffer zone around me was my highest bliss.

The only problem was when people came around. It was so dam aggravating every time, a spiraling down.

That'll never happen to me again--an interruption--cuz I moved on up to a fence and locked gate, hurray.

You can do what you know how to do now. Just act right, stay tidy and speak the truth--WOW!

I'm about to go do what I know how to do. Some last minute things than I'm off to a whole new view.

Women fight thru CALUMNY: reputation-murder. They plant evil seeds against/make em all hate you.

She made everyone hate him and he died in a tiny trailer in the desert. After losing his family he felt cursed.

IT CAN BE DONE. Anything you want that bad is probably destiny and YOU SHALL HAVE IT.

IT'S ALL GOOD

Just go do what you know how to do. C.R. Johnson

A good marriage is like you both have a live-in therapist.

Tucker Carlson's wife never watches the show and doesn't know much about it but it's ok he said.

I grew so tender hearted I couldn't be around anything profane without feeling hurt. William James

If I feel like I'm sixteen why would I wanna hear a buncha ageist projections? They are rudely objectifying.

BAD DEALS

If you keep giving em what they want/not you want they'll continue to leverage down on you and taunt.

Never start relationship on raw deals and if its been that way you gotta say no-deal or life gets unreal.

Instead of trying to make a bad deal work, go find a good deal cuz there's always one out there.

You must find yourself before anyone can find you or to stop chasing other paradigms and people.

Shifting the energy dynamic: You will now put out a more attractive energy/mass attractions will come to you.

A woman feels whole, worthy and complete in a relationship so attractions go UP. Before, not.

If you chase it it means you don't have it. If you have it you'll have that and attract much more to it.

DEPRESSION

Bad psychology causes depression but is exacerbated when the depressed person plays the victim.

IT'S ALL GOOD

You're in a bad state that's all, your depression isn't really "genetic" or clinical you're just irresponsible.

Take ownership of your own psychology cuz most depression comes from arrested development.

It's your software not hardware but people want to point to external problems so they can play the victim.

Much depression is egotism since she's so thoroughly identified with all her many problems.

DEPRESSION IS A BIT NARCISSISTIC

In a big sense, her depression is all about her since she's totally self-absorbed--worrying, panicking and more.

She's thinking about herself and she's depressed. This brings a negative self-image--it just does.

Spirals of negative thinking and deep dark emotions prove to her "there's something wrong with ME."

There's a whole chain of beliefs/assumptions like "I'm not good enough, I need love" feeding low self-worth.

Without personal development there'll be "layers" you're outa touch with and that means depression.

I found out all I needed to know in desert solitude and when people came, I found my lines/what I couldn't do.

Much of the stuff with depression is just BS and past conditioning from traumas or bad breakups.

The mature adult is a self-encourager and Christians have God. There's no reason for depression, just be odd.

Most women are on anti-depressants: they bought the whole line--they can sink in their swill and whine.

IT'S ALL GOOD

These SRI's bloat em up while all creativity stops. A different woman comes out: a depressed cow.

Of course unresolved trauma holds you back, everyone knows that--gotta work on self, drill deep sad sack.

Their feelings of entitlement combined with ingratitude make em depressed: ah, I feel so sorry for em.

NOISE: The depressed are hooked on external stimulation as a compensation and that keeps it going.

COMPENSATORY DEVICES

They're so filled with compensatory devices they can't sit and meditate, drilling way down inside.

Just two seconds in the present moment they see it's not hard/it's actually pleasant and that's the start.

Two seconds in the NOW will prove your natural state is not depressive and your depression is self-generated.

A tiny, tiny minority MAY have a serious condition which is depressive--but it is too rare to even mention.

Root causes of depression: Not living in accord with your core values. Lazy, undisciplined, procrastination.

If you live against your values--you're late, you put things off forever--the result is depression too.

These conflicts may not be causal but feed into it all. Being fake is the biggest cause: you can't walk tall.

A facade is not being honest about your emotions--it's a self-contradiction which brings depression.

Depression comes from people around, mal-adapting to them, trying to please or live up to them.

IT'S ALL GOOD

I'd be joyous in the desert then people-invasion brought depression. It was a reason not a condition.

Living up to other people's standards and expectations--are you kidding? For an adult this is saddening.

Putting up with mindless projections, trivializations or misplaced anger explosions? Depression.

But the minute they were gone I had an **ENLIGHTENING** feeling, a joyous lightening up, a jubilant energy flow.

With this drastic inversion I saw the light--I was meant to be a hermit or just have smart people management.

YOU'RE CREATING THE FEELINGS

Solution: Start noticing how you--thru action or inaction--are creating these feelings and no more blue.

I don't say to meditate, just say look out the window and think, dream, plan vs. how you are blocked by man.

I cannot describe how miserable yours truly was surrounded by people--yet I had no idea, wow.

A shy introvert living in social environment which values conformity over personal autonomy: that was me.

A major result of anti-depressants is more depression.

Firstly, understand what's really important to YOU--it's called values clarification. Now we're cookin'.

If depressed you probably lack **LIFE PURPOSE**. Cuz if you have that there's no way you can be depressed.

Women aren't the problem, it's **LIBERALISM**--but unfortunately most women are liberals.

IT'S ALL GOOD

Women want big government, open borders, unlimited abortion up to birth and anything else weird.

It's not women it's liberalism and feminism in its damaging effect on innocence or dumbness.

If people don't listen to you they don't respect you. This is a major sign but even worse is not valuing your time.

If they come late or not at all you need to set a boundary and ignore their calls--nonverbal signs tell all.

LETTING GO OF PAST

We all have something past that makes us blush, retreat into our shell, cringe, make us feel like hell.

The thing we keep ruminating over is robbing us of energy. It robs our focus too--success isn't coming soon.

The goal: let go of ALL of it. Use the mental trick of putting it all in a bag then throwing the whole thing out.

It can be very hard to let go of it, I know that. But it can also be EASY--don't assume anything else.

To be rid of it fast, see it as a mere concept, just as the future is. It doesn't exist, that's the first.

What a deep thought: I'm putting a huge electrical charge on something that isn't real, not just rot.

The past is dead, just a concept and memory in your head--but now it's tentacles are in the brain instead.

There it sits, those old shits, now how do i get rid of it? It's a start because you just did for two minutes.

BUT you keep bringing it back up and it stays alive by rehearsing your past in your head.

IT'S ALL GOOD

And so you just let it go--very simple--each time it's brought up. It's not hard, simply do it.

Do your introspection, learning from the past, journalizing even writing books about it: but still, forget it.

If you don't consciously let it go it fulfills a self-fulfilling prophesy and some form of it is repeated.

Every time it comes to mind, **CONSCIOUSLY** push it out. You learned from it but now it's time to forget it.

Tell yourself you don't need it anymore, it's not serving you, it's a cancer creating dysfunction, the devil's lore.

You simply **DECIDE** to let go and say "I'm never gonna think about that thing anymore". Be conscious then soar.

PRACTICE LETTING IT GO

Anytime it comes up again--from impulse or habit built up--you cut it off again. Practice doing it again/again.

When an old breakup comes to mind **SUBSTITUTE** with new visions of your future. Practice this over/over.

So you're gonna practice--like a violin: [1] putting it out of mind and [2] substituting with new visions.

Engrave in your mind as if in stone: forget and substitute. See it as a game and you'll win girl/dude.

I'd been caught up in toxic memories for decades and just this simple principal dispersed the clot, ok?

[1] **FORGET** old traumas and divisions and [2] **SUBSTITUTE** with new visions. That's the plan now do em.

Get so busy you don't have time to worry about the past, and **SEE** it as an energy drain not a party blast.

IT'S ALL GOOD

Shamus, Chris, Larry etc. were so horrible they made me into an impenetrable battleship against the rabble.

Go forward to make a million by freely doing your thing established before your birth hon'.

Go do what you know how to do, be great. Just know that old freight will prevent that and the time is late.

EVERY TIME it comes to mind substitute with future glory, riches or fame IF the past is gone/stays behind.

You can do this cuz I did it when so plagued with memories I thought I'd never be free of a past so inveterate.

Spend so much time planning and envisioning your new projects you have NO TIME for the old concepts.

YOU WENT THRU THAT TO BUILD A BATTLESHIP

You went thru that to build your battleship. The foe was your drill instructor and toxic events your bootcamp.

Would you ever tolerate that crap again? Of course not--thus proving how much you learned from it.

I actually thought I could be a friend to youth. I had no idea what they were after the schools screwed em up.

See it as chapters in your book. You've a wealth of knowledge now if with the past you're not hung up.

AVOID LIMITING PEOPLE

In dating relationships, the things you are overlooking now will be amplified later. George Bruno

I'll wait for you forever and you won't see me flirting with others or refusing to wait for birds of a feather.

IT'S ALL GOOD

To them it's not fair that you're progressing in this way and they're not--they need to bring you back down.

If I can shovel negative B.S. so you won't do it, then I don't have to compare myself to you, get it?

People limit you from doing greater things cuz they're not capable of doing it and they can't think ahead.

They're crabs in a bucket cuz they can't have it. You don't deserve anything if they don't--that's it.

Putting insecurities and fears on you means you don't make that jump where suddenly they're just chumps.

The social generation is communistic: SAMENESS. You having something they don't is shameless.

A modern woman jumps into bed as a lark or feather in her cap. If traveling alone she meets a new man for a nightcap.

SEX AND LIBERALS

Making a traveling business hussie stay home just makes her open to neighbors etc. cuz she's never alone.

MOST women today are liberal feminists---isn't that the problem, not women per se?

Homosexuality is part of the depopulation program and that's why they push it: what a scam.

Mommy porn is worse than visual for a highly mental man cuz it opens up windows--make it taboo too.

Liberals have such dirty minds that if you love cats and dogs they assume you're having sex with em.

If I allow you to be free you'll find something better than me so I gotta limit your possibilities, see?

IT'S ALL GOOD

Instead of limiting my freedoms why not focus on making yourself better? That's not ever their thought here.

Successful people don't limit others, they encourage them. Find these kind or your chances are very slim.

Pettifogging: making a big deal of nothing or talking gibberish just to distract from the real thing.

If you know you're amazing you'll encourage others to do the same. But if not, you're gonna be limiting.

If you're fearful/insecure/weak you don't think good things of yourself and you're SURE they'll change up.

Take all that frozen energy in limiting others and put it in yourself instead. Now you both can go ahead.

Now you won't have the time to remember toxic events or limiting those you resent--you're just envisioning.

Now you won't have the time to remember toxic events or limiting those you resent--you have a new bent.

Fear, insecurity, jealousy and weakness is hell to confront. Take em off you like a cloak, now move on up.

Your new focus is on growing, not being limited.

REPLACEABILITY BY NARCISSISTS

ALL people are replaceable to a narcissist--but you can't replace someone special: "interchangeability myth".

This Interchangeability Myth is proven false in Europe. Can the third world replace white Europeans? Hell no.

People and cultures are NOT interchangeable and women aren't either.

A man loves a woman cuz she's irreplaceable. There's something special but a narcissist misses it all.

IT'S ALL GOOD

A narcissist is constantly shifting people. Friends one day, next day not. People are interchangeable--bull!

When I saw how easily Cindy, Winnie or Tom/Dick/Harry could interchange me it was very threatening.

They don't see anything special about you, it's anyone available. This is such an insult--know it girl.

The liberal world thinks everything's replaceable since it's communistic--it's all the same anyway: what bull.

Any man who thinks you're easily replaced I'd escape this minute and NEVER look back--he's a narcissist.

HE THINKS HE CAN REPLACE YOU?

He's the type who would not only go to the next without thought, he'd have sex with her too, a dangerous fop.

He does it to protect from hurt but it makes him ineligible for a classy female who won't be treated like dirt.

This happens because the narcissist doesn't see you are an actual person but a UTILITY with interchangeability.

Just as he replaces a microwave, he can easily replace your function as a utility even if to others you're all the rave.

Replaceability is emotional tragedy cuz we feel it deep inside like when mom replaced us with a new baby.

There are youtube gurus who advise: You don't miss HER you miss her body so simply replace it buddy.

There's many fish in the sea--what an insult, we are unique as snowflakes/God's child so I'd replace the HE.

WHY would a woman want to be with a man who sees her as easily replaced? How cheap--he's a disgrace.

IT'S ALL GOOD

Her personna is SWEET to everyone good or bad--she fails to differentiate so won't defend you from the cad.

"Kindness" is the excuse social justice warriors use when they wanna tyrannize over what people say.

The highest value is TRUTH not "kindness" which is subject to change according to who rules.

HANDLING DISRESPECT

Suddenly someone you care for shows disrespect. You gotta do something lest it cause soul-damage.

Disrespect hurts--it is no small thing. The tragedy is not seeing it while it continues it's down-spiraling.

Disrespect tho' denied comes out in other ways. Depression, physical ailments, loss of destiny.

Disrespect causes heart disease, cancer, panic attacks--from not noticing or protecting yourself against it.

Our spirits were not created to be disrespected and it's a definite breach as our worldview is affected.

We're created for dignity and part of self-love is protecting yourself--the only thing giving back self-respect.

No matter who the person is you gotta get a backbone. Don't be abrasive, just assertive--do it or lose it.

It doesn't matter why they're disrespectful--could be envy. That's not your problem, don't question it sweetie.

The only thing we can control is who we're around/who we let in. It's a boundary issue now: limit them.

I was rejuvenated and renewed by walking away from disrespect. I had taken it but now I'm back.

IT'S ALL GOOD

It takes **SKILL** to discern and walk away--but it strengthens your identity as a child of God immediately.

It takes skill to recognize disrespect/skill to walk away from it but opens us up to new horizons/lovingness.

So you over-react at times--don't fall into the trap of that justifying their disrespect or risk down-spiraling.

Their disrespect is a character issue so it's nothing you can change, all you can do is set boundaries or be blue.

Try to change the disrespect through self-improvement and it exacerbates their envy, just sayin'.

RECOGNIZE—OR IT MAGNIFIES

If you don't recognize it due to past conditioning the disrespect magnifies since you don't respect self.

Character doesn't change--it stays static. Protect yourself to make sure it doesn't happen again/be adamant.

If you detect a pattern of disrespect and let it continue that is totally degrading to you--you're unequal.

Perhaps they don't have the skills to respect you. Tough--you still must escape the scene or be blue.

You can keep em as acquaintance but letting em close is self-abandonment--If it's sister forget family dinners.

Above all, respect your intuition. If it's diffident about facing em again, don't go and just love your own.

If one feels nervous during holidays, ask why? Once you spend em with friends and pets you'll feel high.

Saying **NO** to boundary-busters and disrespecters starts a whole new life of self-love with destiny makers.

IT'S ALL GOOD

If censured at family dinners they're disrespecting you. Be around people loving what you say or be blue.

We have a god-given right to freely live without people controlling our words-- no more family dinners.

I didn't know this fantastic information that I've a right to be respected or that life without it would be so wrecked.

CANNIBUS: AWAY WITH YA'

Pot opened up windows in my mind. As a philosopher, thinker, writer/whatever, this was a real find.

But there comes a time when all "good" things must come to an end. I stopped cold so I could breathe again.

I coughed as much as Hillary Clinton and it was darn embarrassin'. So glad I stopped my pot smokin'.

I'd take walks at 3 am in the dark, breathing hard and praying for regeneration tho' lungs were scarred.

When it came time to stop, praying for God's help, I never wanted it again. With each breath I was on the mend.

After decades it wasn't doing anything anyway, just an empty habit--this awareness was crucial, ok?

The herb: I really believe it opened windows in my mind but to my poor scarred lungs it was SO unkind.

I was self-congratulatory for years, saying "it isn't tobacco" as if it was morally superior--what a debacle.

Just as it's becoming legal I was letting it go. I think back to what I went thru to get it from dark fellows.

How I put myself in danger to get it--just about do anything for it--for insights making the world more fit.

IT'S ALL GOOD

I saw all the appurtenances--pipes, lighters, pipe cleaners--and threw em all away. Felt like a child again, ok?

I saw pot-smoking cessation as the biggest achievement of my lifetime--more than degrees, books, anything.

I learned what I learned--going deep inside, the isolation aside--but this season was over: in joy I cried.

Every time the hippie Hillary Clinton coughs for the world to see, I feel so grateful I got out so lungs can breathe.

No edibles either--the quickest way to the ER for sensitives like me, triggering psychoses/terror/feeling crappy.

Just to be normal like a child--realizing I wasn't taking anything to get there--made me feel beguiled.

That feeling of guilt-free normalcy was the new "high" for me. I was disgusted with the coughing, you see.

COUGH TILL IT'S GONE

The flu released coughing to clear the lungs and I took advantage of this. Black stuff gone = bliss.

I walk two brisk miles at 3 am and with each breath I think: I'm getting well, I'm not gonna die with this stink.

It's the flu I have to thank for the END--it was the releasing mechanism and I'm not filling my lungs up again.

I still see it as a necessary phase, I was "legal" I'd say--but it's over now and a forgiving God said I'd be ok.

I don't drink/rarely eat so I saw myself as a saint despite a habit which for an old lady was "quaint".

More than education and books written this was my biggest accomplishment: stoppin' pot smokin'.

IT'S ALL GOOD

The cure: LOVE your lungs, feel sorry for them, care for them like a sick child ready to die, cry for them.

The heart and lungs are vital organs man and by smokin' you cut your life short--accept it, stop it now go on.

Stopping pot smoking: biggest revolution in my life. My lungs were destroyed but I think they're comin' back.

For the first time in decades I'm not coughing. I prayed God would remove craving and it's a good thing.

I thank God I'm not coughing anymore. Flu or not, it was the pot. Old hippies unite: keep that curse out!

The pot from dispensaries is not like the old days. They say it's way stronger but to me, it's just blase.

I used to think of pot as insights, relief, attitude adjustment. Now when I think of it I only recall the COUGH.

UNACKNOWLEDGED SIGNS OF DISRESPECT

If the signs of disrespect are ignored/aren't felt it duplicates your past. Bring it to awareness and fight back!

If someone lies/withholds information it's disrespectful. Lock em down, get away: now be grateful.

I just always had a bad feeling in my heart about him/her/them. That was disrespect man.

It's the unacknowledged feelings of disrespect that kill the spirit/murder the soul--you feel obsolete and old.

Devaluation--of your needs, looks, body, works, thoughts--is disrespectful and you better start noticing girl.

If it means you never go to family dinners again, good. You've now achieved what only saints could.

IT'S ALL GOOD

My dear mother got so nervous with holidays. It's cuz the folks came around and **REALLY** made her pay.

They'd bring up stuff that happened in the past. Who needs this? The holidays were a pissing contest.

Mom felt the signs of disrespect but would drink over it. Face em--become **AWARE** of em--then forget it.

It's the victims of disrespect who use addictions to deal with the tension, thus sealing their lower station.

With addictions, what came first--the disrespect or the crutch? Quit and see for it doesn't matter much.

Devaluing means disrespecting. Worthy criticism is one thing but condescending is crippling.

Our model for dealing with disrespect is our wonderful President Trump. Despite all he remains on top.

It's up to you to put a stop to devaluation the minute you recognize it-- immediately you feel **ENLIGHTENMENT**.

Don't be afraid to stand up for yourself by simply walking away gently. Don't lose it all by becoming angry.

THE SILENT TREATMENT

The silent treatment: They no longer respond after you set a boundary. This is obvious disrespect honey.

When I set a boundary she got mad/withdrew completely. All I asked was that you call first sweetie.

People withdraw to protect themselves for some reason. So I took a look at that and then moved on.

I have boundaries and won't let you in just because you came to the door. This isn't the fifties you know.

IT'S ALL GOOD

The silent treatment, withdrawing, being neglectful: is it you, or are they disrespectful? Balance is all.

The silent treatment always gets you wondering: Is it something I've done, am I to blame? Think.

Silence opens so many questions and that's why I hate it but that's what they want so learn to ignore it.

Silence is disrespect cuz it says "I don't have to talk to you and I don't really want to." So glad I'm free of you.

I got it from my mother, I got it from my sisters. At this stage of the game I won't put up with you either.

A LOVER WON'T PLAY GAMES

If someone respects you they can't wait to talk to you. If ignored, get away quick/feel relief [whew].

Yes you have given me the silent treatment. That's your rudder of control used in the past--admit it.

Obviously physical abuse is disrespect--but busting your boundaries is definitely a form of that.

I set boundaries with Shane but he kept coming back. When I'd withdraw he'd come closer--this is disrespect.

Some women feel aroused by boundary-busters moving in--is it heightened interest or did it just trigger em?

Boundary-busting is serious. Gotta keep your physical boundaries in place or pay the dire consequences.

Are they working or going to school? No they're coming around to waste your time cuz they're cool.

Slander/gossip from Cindy showed absolute disrespect but I never confronted her cuz she'd just do it more.

IT'S ALL GOOD

I was apprehensive to confront gossip cuz I knew she'd never stop--she'd get on the phone to keep it up.

They break a boundary then act real innocent. If you give in get ready for the explosion that's imminent.

You explained it once, if they don't understand tough luck. Don't keep wasting time with a user, buck up.

If they don't listen to your concerns that's disrespect. If it's "but I don't understand" it doesn't matter, defect.

If they dismiss your concerns or ignore them, that is disrespect. Learn this thoroughly or good luck.

SET A BOUNDARY BABY

If you set a boundary that makes em mad and they come back and you let em in, you've had it.

Before I was married I was a sitting duck for disrespecters. The spouse is the wall/marriage fences her.

Forcing their values on you is disrespectful. Whether right or wrong thoy're saying your life falls below.

I lived like a monk loving the Lord but they came around telling me to go to church. Stand up/take charge.

I gained worlds studying the bible in my cabin. Going to church was so boring since they started falling.

Church ladies would come around bitchin' cuz I wasn't a part of em. This is disrespect/I was way above em.

Unsolicited advice is disrespect. I got this when from society I defected then gained strength against it.

I don't like thinking back cuz it stirs anxiety/makes me mad--but with constant disrespect I almost collapsed.

IT'S ALL GOOD

You share your vulnerabilities and they hop on with criticizing. Recognize they are disrespecting.

If you're an adult you need to make your own decisions. Wise counsel is one thing but they're just fishin'.

If he won't take responsibility for his actions against you, that is disrespect. Making commands is also it.

He pushes your buttons with sting-shots and roundabouts. He makes you jealous intentionally: get him out.

He pushes buttons that [you know he knows] trigger and bother you. Kick him to the curb, start anew.

He asks inappropriate questions not his business. Feel it, know it--be fearless, have wiseness.

THE DUKE AND DUCHESS

Democrats are a broken record. It's an old false narrative [shove-down] striking a chord but makes us bored.

Meghan insisted on leaving "racist" country Britain. By the mean things they said about her it was proven.

She doesn't have all-white skin, that's why they didn't like her. And Harry went along with it, good luck Sir.

Though they treated her like royalty that wasn't enough cuz they opened their mouths against her stuff.

Meghan was a victim of "racism" which forced her to move to Canada, and stoked Harry went along with ya'.

Their wedding cost citizens a fortune and they were gifted an amazing mansion but still it was "racism".

She was treated like a princess and lived in luxury at the taxpayers expense but all that's irrelevance.

IT'S ALL GOOD

The UK bends over backwards for ethnic minorities and thus Meghan's cries of racism are selfish/silly.

Was Harry just a stepping stone to her greater success? She married a royal, knowing all the drawbacks.

The UK turns a blind eye to crimes committed by minorities against whites. But they're racist Meghan griped.

The victims of ethnic crimes are of British descent--but Meghan complains she's the one they all resent.

THE UK IS RACIST MEGHAN SAYS

Men from ethnic minorities raped 20,000 children of British descent. UK is "racist" tho' there was no punishment.

All crimes against whites were covered over by the British establishment but they're "racist", imagine that.

The children were abused in plain sight of the Manchester police--but the UK is racist Meghan Markel says.

The child rapists are always "Asian men"--like it was by someone from China, Korea, Taiwan or Japan.

When UK girl was raped by 500 men by eleven she was the one charged for prostitution. UK = racism?

The mass rape covered up by a deluge of pointless gossip about a washed up divorced actress tells the most.

Stories of evil white racists is top news but ethnic child rapists are hidden behind Meghan Markle's blues.

VICTIMS of racism are the indigenous peoples and by that I don't mean Indians but the whites-called-evil.

Are you blocked or is it the silent treatment? Figure that out then do your business/don't be pushed.

IT'S ALL GOOD

I love you/you love me but honey there's nothing we can do with this situation so I'm letting you go, be free.

We don't always get what we want in life. I wanna do wrong/it feels so right so I'll pray for God's light.

You're so worthless he was able to let you go easily. Does that make him a strong man or weaselly?

He's just going thru different phases to learn. That's how we mature--ten up, five back, just persevere.

Blacks didn't show at Virginia's protest for gun rights, it was only whites--so now they call guns racist alright?

White care about self-defense you know, but that's called an "outbreak of terrorism on American soil."

If you're hooked telepathically don't do anything wrong or he'll pick up on it baby.

I pray for help every day of my life. I'm weak, He's not; I'm befuddled, He knows all; He's kind/I'm in strife.

THE NEW AGE AIN'T SAGACIOUS

The new destroyers: define those doing worse as victims and define those doing better as perpetrators.

Their thinking is so impaired by a generation of lies they're incapable of seeing the truth/can't help but despise.

He was a "humble" man but he said it in such a way that his humility made him better than you: liberal blues.

Narcissistic gush period is shorter/discard comes sooner. Just by your reciprocation you scared em dear.

When you become [so soon] "too much" they just naturally distance themselves and shut down: yuk!

IT'S ALL GOOD

But the discard should bring you supreme elation. No more ups and downs, wondering, deflation.

Now you put the energy back on yourself to the wonderment of who YOU are without this scar.

How many times have you played this game and been ensnared in emotional ups/downs and pain?

The pain comes from your focus on HIM/HER rather than yourself. Put it back: be elated as the magic elf.

One of the bountiful rewards of refocusing is never thinking about em again. The relief is a WIN.

Once you're outa their spin it's SO MUCH FUN. Like a child again: this was just a weary side trip friend.

HE PUTS YOU THRU THE RINGER

Once free of his zingers you realize he put you through the ringer and you're so glad it's over!

For you're a child of God and deserve consistent love. That's as God wants it, not way up and down.

They love you so much, see? Then suddenly you're clingy, you want too much, you're suffocating me.

Since you couldn't make a move without criticism, now you're free of them you can express your gems.

You see now the very things they criticized were things they did constantly: you're done with hypocrisy.

Notice how they never gave you credit when it was due—but would reward someone else in full view.

Now you're free you'll gain no more masochistic pleasure from their sadistic teasers--that's leisure.

IT'S ALL GOOD

Who did they think they were, bashing you for the very things they did constantly? Try to forget sweetie.

You were nervous in the relationship knowing every move you made was going to be criticized publicly.

They weren't one-tenth what you are, but in this system you came out below par and they were the star.

Stay home, pull back into your comfy situation and thank God you got out in time to share these rhymes.

In a very short time they ghost or slow fade you and you think "it wasn't real"--but it was, he's just a scuzz.

The thrill is gone. The classic response of all narcissism survivors is: "I'm so glad it's over, what a joker'.

Prepare for him/her to circle back over. Knowing that's a pattern will arm you when it happens: be clever.

They're fascinated but then you reciprocated and they felt suffocated: Recall this pattern to not be deflated.

Let someone else be his victim, you're done with him. Let them go up and down and end up maudlin.

You will always end up saying: Who was he to criticize me when he was doing the exact same things?

Return to God, your Father. He loves you and everything about you for He made you. Not this buffoon.

In just retribution, take on the narcissist pattern: You felt that about him but now you don't, bye bye chum.

SOCIAL MEDIA AND THE NARCISSIST

The narcissist loves social media: it's his ultimate playground as he plays multiple fools at once.

IT'S ALL GOOD

Part of going no-contact is NEVER, EVER going to their page or somehow you'll be punched in the face.

You be the king/queen of your own domain and never visit their shit realm again or you'll start a decline.

They'll incite jealousy with others or post statements of passive-aggression and you don't need it hon'.

When you're tempted to go to their page, ask yourself: Do I wanna be punched in the face today?

Knowing his patterns do you good or go backwards: Everything is manipulation: be forewarned.

Go to his page: question yourself and feel bad. Stay away: continue your feelings of joy, rid of this cad.

Everything that is posted is contrived to manipulate somebody. Keep this in mind, avoid a tragedy.

Everything he says is wrong but sounds good. You know this but repressed it about his heart of wood.

If you ever saw his inbox there'd be lies, triangulations, manipulations with everyone. Be rid of him!

You going to his/her page is self-destruction just like going back to drugs. See it that way, avoid this thug.

NARCISSISTS AND SOCIAL MEDIA

Never allow a narcissist to use social media as a tool of manipulation--awaken! Be smarter than.

If only to get you back into their ring, they'll say something good and you'll be down in the mud again.

Be smarter than the narcissist. I've given you the tools--just know their patterns then do what you need to.

IT'S ALL GOOD

How long were you up and down? A week, a month? You got off easy, don't waste any more time sweetie.

Whenever you feel smitten again, think of their inbox: you think it's empty my friend? Not a chance.

Just don't look--erase it from your mind, get into other things--avoid crooks, there's a million books.

If he's a huge social media presence he's probably a narcissist esp. if unexplained [he's not the best].

Wake up on this: A huge social media presence but he's not famous--there's manipulation, he's a narcissist.

WALK AWAY AND MEAN IT

If he's done something no self-respecting person would put up with you gotta walk away and mean it.

Come-here-go-away relationships are intolerable. You must walk away and mean it to go on again.

People who can't walk away are seen as so pathetic and weak: picture it as if it's yourself, and SPLIT!

Who would respect someone who [thinking they can do no better] would put up with this nut you're nuts over?

Who wants a partner who is so low-value, low confidence they'd stay with a loser like this? Get a life miss.

Never be part of his inbox where he can pick and choose. You're not his muse, he's just using you.

He's the downside of the computer world, now go to the upside: find worthy mentors, now be much better.

Imagine a washed up masochist where you could do anything to them and they'll still kiss your ass!

IT'S ALL GOOD

GREATNESS WALKS AWAY BABY

You can measure your greatness by your ability to walk away. That marks a winner--remember this, ok?

You can be successful/an overachiever but let me say a mouthful: If you can't walk away it's all downhill.

He was just another chapter in your book about disaster and as it happens it made him more attractive.

When they do something bad you must walk away and **NEVER TALK TO THEM AGAIN**. Are you in, friend?

If you can't do that--if you say in the ring with this creepy thing--what does that say about you, darling?

You act so strong and confident--but it means nothing because staying with him makes you a has-been.

The narcissist won't change. Never, ever forget that or get worse and worse until you're totally deranged.

Your confidence, strength and courage is a dam lie if you stay with something that is so confusing.

What is he/she anyway? No one's that great. If it had been God's will it would never hurt this way. Ready? OK!

WORKING ON YOURSELF ALWAYS WORKS

Working on yourself always works: there's no downside and you become so much happier free of jerks.

Tell the truth but "don't hurt their feelings". What a bunch of hogwash/new age falsehood. Say it/mean it.

You don't need him for all will want you soon cuz you've disentrenched from falsehood and this goon.

IT'S ALL GOOD

Look forward with glee to the future when free. Know it's a love addiction when smitten with a creep.

Make yourself more interesting by pursuing things that interest YOU. More creativity or athleticism dude.

Pursue your OWN interests then you'll attract the same to you, not this confusing and hurtful indifference.

Now go on to a glorious future. It was just a slight misadventure but you learned so much it was worth it.

Think of all your great ancestors, so proud you were able to overcome this character so phony and loud.

I love music, philosophy/psychology, political events, home remodeling, pet darlings and I attract the same to me.

PURSUE WHAT YOU LIKE

Don't pursue what "they" say you should--go to gym, losing ten pounds--but what YOU like, that's good.

If you do what others think you should it's just work, a chore to please someone else. Express your SELF.

I'm interested right now in landscaping my property and am attracting artistic folk who want to help me.

Get into THAT then ATTRACT that. Amazing isn't it how it works: don't pursue anyone just be a bad ass.

The sweet little cute lady said "I don't give a dam what you think old man" and she was free, just like that.

By far the greatest release for me is music and creativity. It's so boundless I'm off to a whole new destiny.

I'm telling you love addiction--to PEOPLE--is creepier than a substance cuz your loving God doesn't want this.

IT'S ALL GOOD

If you wanna travel, be a gypsy, climb mountains--do it. I just wanna stay in my lovely home and think about it.

Whatever interests you, do it. He's not part of it--you've overvalued something you need to be rid of.

Like attracts like and the more you get into THOSE areas the more successful you'll be in all endeavors.

Your loving God didn't make you to pursue creeps to make you whole. HE makes you whole/He's got a plan doll.

LIKE LIKES LIKE

If you wanna meet an ambitious person, be ambitious. The level you reach will attract the same, not a leech!

I went thru this, I overcame this and God-willing you can too miss. When you think of him, substitute with God.

If you're a celebrity actor, go with a celebrity actor. Don't choose the camera guy you think may be safer.

I guarantee one thing: When you get away from this situation you may even hate him--a new beginning.

What separates the great from everyone else is their ability to block the real world out.

This guy has been a thorn in your side from day one. So this is your definitive test--can you let him go hon'?

It's the test of your resolve. With God everything is a test or reward--will you pass it and go fast forward?

Will you do your destiny and go forward, or fall back into your addiction to a narcissist, an attention whore?

Don't ever hop on someone else's train. It's so self-deprecating you'll go insane. Focus: avoid pain.

IT'S ALL GOOD

Never feel angry at the past's lessons that got you to here. They were necessary or you'd still be back there.

CORONAVIRUS

The coronavirus was caused by snakes--never mind the 2018 patent by Bill and Melinda Gates.

Virus scare at LAX, Texas/Chicago/Europe hit, 40 million quarantined and it's caused by snakes? NOT LEGIT.

So, the FDA has approved a vaccine for the coronavirus just as it comes out-- what a coincidence, no?

Coronavirus' origins as a bio-engineered weapon is proven by animal-to-human transmission. Mike Adams

Diseases with the highest fatality rates also have the shortest incubation but that's been reversed now.

The anti-human biochemists made coronavirus with longer incubation so symptoms are silent until they hit.

Coronavirus will now be the go-to lever to declare lockdown of all our cities as they take over.

Virus vaccines: They will use the virus for every single narrative of blame to make us give up all our rights.

The virus will provide the pretext for major crackdowns and predictably this will involve our guns.

The feces-strewn sewer cities will be the first to go with the coronavirus. They're RIPE for a huge mess.

The biosludge vector can be easily used to weaponize and depopulate. The city puts in on our farms, ok?

Biosludge Definition: Feces, urine, viruses and drugs melted down to use as fertilizer--we're done.

IT'S ALL GOOD

Every leftist city is an open sewer. Most are leaving Austin cuz as liberals say "pooping is freedom" sir.

Left's lovely plan: Open borders, let everyone in, eliminate health screening, make your city an open sewer.

With the city's sludge we're primed to get hit fast. Make no mistake: crapping in the open air is a speedy virus.

The priorities of liberals are devastating. They're against using straws but ok with dangerous street-pooping.

LIBERAL POOPING IN THE CITY

The software model predicting 65 million dead globally didn't add in the viruses from CITY FECES.

How did Bill and Melinda Gates war game this 3 months ago, and even patent the virus, ya know?

The globalists always say beforehand what they're gonna do. It's in their papers and conventions too.

The alternative to wining/dining scientists is to say "you do this or you're dead--it's best for you family, 'nuf said".

The fact they're doing all this right now means they're going for broke against the president--it's real.

The coronavirus is obviously a prepared simulant cuz they have other stuff that's even worse to implement.

Alex Jones scared me 15 years ago but it's so much worse than he said: they've made their move/we're dead.

They've taken over every institution--media, colleges, major corporations--so it's going forth, son.

We're not just screwed we're targeted for extermination. A planned wipeout of humanity is on the horizon.

IT'S ALL GOOD

Mass censorship is just surface layer to shut our mouths so their attacks can succeed and we're wiped out.

The viciousness of their attacks proves they're desperate to pull out all the stops--from impeachment to this.

The CDC has been taken over by the vaccine industry--telling more than a library of books unfortunately.

The coronavirus is simply the first wave. The second wave is the dangerous packed-with-crap vaccines, ok?

Expect LIVE VIRUS in the coronavirus vaccine: beyond world wars, a catastrophe like we've never seen.

IT'S ALL BEEN PLANNED

This has already been planned/engineered. So sorry to tell you this but please wake-up and prepare dear.

Food and masks are already sold out. I bought dozens of mask after Bill Gates gave his talk. Store food NOW.

Liberals aren't our friends but our foes. Open borders, open sewers: imagine the catastrophe then GO.

The masses will be slaughtered because the depopulation agenda can NOT BE STOPPED. Listen up!

Get outa the cities, NOW! Or be locked down and you'll never get out. Hear these words, GO: Ciao!

We're all targeted for termination and only lone survivors will be left. Store food, water, bandages, masks.

Stop lazy complacency. Watch WWII docs where millions were killed and other catastrophes from history.

I've read hundreds of history books. Most history is catastrophe--it's the human condition sorry to say.

IT'S ALL GOOD

Most will naively ignore coronavirus--this bioengineered weapon system now being delivered to us.

They engineered this virus so it can't be identified until it's too late: no symptoms are seen until bad fate.

Since doctors can't diagnose, diseased patients fall thru the cracks and when scanned, "you don't have it".

The WHO [world health organization] downplays it. Of course they do--they're all part of it.

PEOPLE ARE DROPPING DEAD

People are dropping dead on streets of China. Supplies have run out, they're selling used masks: God come!

As cities are quarantined food supplies run out immediately. Get prepared, buy freezers, stay free.

As Big Pharma has taken over China, Chinese medicine or natural cures like colloidal silver are banned.

Why is that? Because they can't have people cured or surviving what's been engineered to kill them.

Their own simulations funded by Bill and Melinda Gates show 65 million will be killed, ok?

Their software predictions vastly underestimate the filthy conditions in our cities, an imminent tragedy.

They don't include the recycling of biosludge from human feces and putting it on our farm's food supply.

Imagine the devastation when it's found our food supply is contaminated with the virus--and it WILL BE.

Your food ends in feces, it becomes biosludge and will be transported out to the farms from the cities.

IT'S ALL GOOD

In Washington state they just legalized dissolved human corpses to be used as fertilizer, I'm not lying here.

Instead of burying/cremation they DISSOLVE em in chemicals/flush em down the city sewer system.

Dead people who coulda died from coronavirus can now be in the biosludge fertilizing our food farms. ALARM!

Understand: in Washington/Oregon/California they'll vaccinate you at gunpoint--it's part of the plan.

Bill and Melinda Gates are the science officers for this plan, that's all on record so you'd better prepare man.

It's very difficult for most to truly comprehend the scale of what's happening. Soylent green was people.

MARTIAL LAW AND QUARANTINE TRAINING

Quarantine training is taking place. Yes to contain the virus but MOSTLY to lock us down then KILL US.

They poison everything and kill the earth while saying they wanna save it. Contradictions define things like this.

They wine and dine their science collaborators and then to destroy the evidence they kill em. I may be one.

The in-your-face blatant criminality and insane lawlessness is a shit test to see what they can get away with.

Most cancer viruses breed in feces. San Francisco is awash in it/you step in it: expect mass disease.

Cancer comes from viruses--that's a well known fact--and viruses come in vaccines, packed with crap.

Their worldview is they're gonna be superscientists that rule the earth, transcending their human form.

IT'S ALL GOOD

It's a eugenics cult buying off the scientific community thru recruitment, money, power--and then compromise.

The fingerprints of Bill and Melinda Gates and the UN are all over the coronavirus "project" in a PATENT.

Jeffrey Epstein was a FRONT MAN for nefarious science projects of the globalists--compromising scientists.

Especially biochemists are seduced, groomed, wined and dined, sent on vacations and bought mansions.

What Ph.D. wouldn't get a big head over that? They feel it's their own empire they're creating: FAT CATS.

They torture live animals for their evil projects but the vegans don't object--they worry over pronouns.

Bill Gates was on PBS saying we must depopulate and he's patented thru a subgroup called coronavirus, ok?

It's ok if millions are killed because it brings in WORLD GOVERNMENT: communism/taking the guns.

HIX POLITIX

"I was simply stunned by the masses of white men carrying guns." That's all you hear on fake news in sum.

If blacks kill each other by the dozen that's ok, we'll forget em. But if whites walk with guns we're gonna get em.

Northern Virginia has changed from mass immigration--so much that when voting there's no republican option.

"2nd amendment supporters are unstable and mentally ill" they say and that's how they think increasingly.

Bloomberg promises to triple black wages in the next decade. That sounds like reparations to me.

IT'S ALL GOOD

They arrest Owen Shroyer for wearing an innocent sign but let anti-Trumpers protest and run around wild.

The extraordinarily awful things happening every hour are not committed by our ancestors from the Mayflower.

No I don't want floods of people with brutal customs coming here, why would any one sir?

Joe Biden is a pedo the media refuses to topple.

Deep state is bigger than Trump having been implanted on every level by Obama, like liberal judges.

I love living in cowboy country, called "fly over" by the liberal nut jobs from coastal cities.

LIBERALS HATE CONSERVATIVES

Liberals hate conservatives or haven't you noticed? Does this explain the trouble you've had with relatives?

We want the proliferation of white babies so get busy.

Trump planned to de-escalate Russia while withdrawing from Middle Eastern wars--going against dem lores.

Nothing made them hate him more than these two things-- going against their leftist narrative, dogma, ideas.

Goldman Sachs is feeding the mob in the hopes they'll eat them last. Tucker Carlson

Feces and needles everywhere: liberal cities are open sewers as they open borders and don't care.

The deep state pretends its the savior when it's actually behind the whole operation, and it's big man.

The spirit of the second amendment has nothing to do with sport. It's an equalizing force for free souls.

IT'S ALL GOOD

Everything is Trump's fault/Trump can do no wrong: these are the two strains of the derangement syndrome.

The rejection of the moral order of the created universe results in radical evil--Germany's legalizing it all.

Germany: licentiousness is the new morality of the secular materialist establishment and homeschool is illegal.

RACE REALISM

Every race has it's pros and cons. White race built Europe cuz they think abstractly and have imagination.

Though Asians have higher IQ than whites they lack imagination/abstract thinking which is limiting.

Some are so dam dumb it isn't funny with a propensity to violence. It takes high IQ to have self-constraint.

Some are musical, some aren't, some are balancers, etc. This is called race realism but libs call it "racism".

Of course we're talking about AVERAGES. Some escape the bell shaped curve of the other savages.

Let's face it: the Nigerians didn't build Europe. They didn't have the same skills. The white man did.

If they coulda built Europe why do they come from S-hole countries? It's a different IQ/skill set I tell you.

The white race builds comfortable, safer societies so they all wanna come here--that always happens for sure.

When men cease to believe in God they do not believe in nothing, but are capable of believing anything.

MORE THOUGHTS ON IT

IT'S ALL GOOD

I didn't feel good on crackers and butter. Judge food by how you feel [light, quick, energetic] to be better.

Even though I'm very small if it comes from China I must buy extra-large or even ex/ex large that's all.

Humans are incredibly toxic compared to wild animals and their corpses are going into the food supply now.

Wild animals eat wild food while humans eat poison-inundated crops making us sick, fat, screwed.

Human corpse sludge transported to America's food crops and this they're calling "green" from the rooftops.

The only way to control sleep apnea [choking] without that tiresome clumsy mask is to not eat past breakfast.

Waking up choking is TERRIFYING: you're facing death every time. Nothing in alimentary canal, I'm fine.

Energize thru temperance: Dissipation and excess always leads to defeat, boredom, depression, tiredness.

IT'S ALL GOOD?

The sweet lady survivor said: I wanna be nice and good but am so afraid of the rage inside.

Everywhere is the rot of aimlessness/watching TV all day. IQ and brainwaves dropping, humanity is dying.

I don't write unless it first comes thru mind. I'm a slave to it--writer's block was never a problem of mine.

I write from midnight to noon. Who does that unless it's a destiny worthy of success, and soon?

I wanna go on and succeed in a bright new cosmic plan not repeat and dredge up these dreary dragons.

IT'S ALL GOOD

INEVITABILITY OF LIFE

There's an obvious inevitability to life, the handwriting is on the wall. I can see it and you can too y'all.

Just accept what's happening and go with the flow. You don't like changes but it's basic to life ya' know.

It gives me hope that you can see it too. Life is strange isn't it but things will be better for me and you.

The best neighborhood possible: No one ever bothers you but they'd be there for you in an emergency, no?

If I fight circumstances I get nervous but if I just trust and go with what I THINK is happening it's glorious.

Changes are happening and there's not a thing I can do to stop em. Gotta go with it with joy/God has a plan.

If I choose to stop the change, it's sad and futile. If I choose to accept the inevitable, I'll be able.

Go with the change because things are always better with God. That's unless you're a sinner, not just flawed.

I wish I could get thru the transition, but things take time. Or a miracle could happen and all could realign.

Thank you for your patience--it's God's greatest attribute. Natural change is unfoldment, it's just evolution.

Warning: Get outa the cities there's gonna be race wars, pandemics, starvation, Martial Law and gungrabbing.

After a thorough and studied investigation I found a safe place. I moved, I did it: I geographically relocated.

Once I found the right place I saved my money then got the hell out. Since then California's gone to pot/rot.

IT'S ALL GOOD

RELOCATION THE GREATEST ACCOMPLISHMENT

Relocating was my greatest accomplishment in life. I don't feel scared anymore as I did in police state California.

And I don't wanna be anywhere near a city, for most are liberal. That means shit-holes, corrupt as hell.

I did it, I'm safe and can relax now. Middle America is real folks and the pretty red mountains are all around.

My name was Maria Civetta meaning a wise old owl. Then I changed it to Karen Kellock, that's all I know.

There's nothing wrong with the woman leading at times. She leads the way and he sees it as sublime.

It happens that way at times, don't get upset. Sometimes the woman knows what's best, now be blessed.

If it's God's plan you gotta be patient. Let things happen as they wilt--don't push it--and you'll be amazed.

So he's a dam narcissist, aren't we all? Much narcissism is self-protective from prior hurt, just ask God.

It's two houses on an acre housing me/you, two kittens, an old wise cat and two dogs who just wanna play ball.

In a country neighborhood it's like a big family. They're always there for you but understand my solitude.

GO WHERE THE COWS WALK BY

Cows walk by weekly/they stop when they see me. Ranchers aren't gonna sell so we'll stay like this, free.

When I decided where to go I put "house for sale" in the search/up came the best in the whole area, I swear.

IT'S ALL GOOD

God is so good if you're living right but so mean and wrathful if you're not--believe this or go to rot.

God ain't always loving like new agers say. He disciplines as He sees fit and we love Him that way.

So that's all I gotta say, that's the plan. As things heat up--as they WILL--you may get gumption to come along.

You've heard of heroes without a country: "no man knows my history" for there's too much complexity.

NO ONE KNOWS MY HISTORY

And I prefer it that way. You geographically relocate then that's it, no history--no need to go back, you're free.

But was it "all good"? Hell no! Much of it was terrible--that's how I learned I was happy to be alone.

So I'm just gonna relax now that you got my message. I had to tell you and these 110 books are my legacy.

The winds come up every afternoon, they sing thru tho window. Crickets at night, roosters in the morning.

I'm telling your there's no place like it. A country neighborhood not a ranch, we need protection.

Not a track development--boring! But a bunch of houses all with land, with utterly beautiful surroundings.

Ok now that the truth is out I won't worry anymore. That's such a relief, I can just enjoy the day and explore.

THEN JUST THINK, YOU'LL RISE UP

Fame solves shame problem. You're ABOVE the friggin' herd that thinks it's so superior but is wrong.

IT'S ALL GOOD

Since only a genius can know a genius, persecution is certain in a fallen world/drought of nothingness

No matter how weaselly she is [shrew] give Jezebel a little power and she always abuses it over you.

It's whatever God wants. I believe He does have a plan and when you fail a plan B, even better than.

An acre can be a network of charming nooks and crannies or a junk yard of clutter of losers and meanies.

Disorder/clutter is so low-class. No matter how modest your circumstances you can still be aristocrat.

AOC: Good people hate the commie witch you see. Shamelessly she's trying to destroy the country.

Crappy childhood attachments destroy early life but show up later in depression and we don't know why.

If weakened in addiction one may succumb to the control of previous/bad systems, a real predicament.

EVERLASTING JOY NOT LUXURY

A real woman seeks everlasting joy not temporary luxury. Dinners, events are over but I live in eternity.

A real woman never settles for less not cuz she's proud but because she knows her worth/of God.

When a boy dates a real woman he says "she's arrogant and hard to handle": boy, skedaddle.

A genius can argue subjects he knows nothing about cuza one tiny detail from which he logics everything out.

Is he a real man or a dangerous boy? Dangerous boys demand, take, intimidate/are easily annoyed.

IT'S ALL GOOD

A major cause of divorce is a wife's girlfriends: they never take his side and divorce is recommended.

ChiComs mad at Kim Jun Un for making deals with Trump so they took him out/put his sister up.

ChiComs will make it all trendy: Oh we have a woman dictator now and isn't she cute/friendly.

Attachment/trauma bonds are the GIST of the new psychology which is a systems approach.

It's a constant problem keeping others away and carving out our own destiny--ALONE is the only way.

Any woman seeking her unique identity--the hero's path or philosopher's stone--they see as enemy.

It's like the entire town took me on for the sin of wanting to be SEPARATE and alone, seen as arrogant.

THE RIGHT TO LIVE YOUR OWN LIFE

We're banned from groups for being too intellectual, discerning and complex called "troublemaking".

I didn't have a right to live my own life, have my own instincts or speak my mind--these were crimes.

I'm Number One to you or forget it. You can't put me on their level that's a dam insult and I feel it.

It's not that they wouldn't let me work but I couldn't have the LUXURY of being alone, not under their gun.

A man alone is seen as a nerd into his own thing. A woman alone is seen as hideous or a hussy.

The internet is infinite, I'm not gonna light on you any longer. Just the thought of it is a bummer.

IT'S ALL GOOD

The social generation is our biggest obstruction. People used to be humble, discrete, quiet, homebound.

Must learn to push it back in his face not take the blame--that's the old systems model.

Porn is cheating, period. All other arguments are irrelevant distractions. Transcend details/just realize that.

Outer trappings of success combined with lack of self-awareness thru social hypnotics is sickness.

SYSTEMS MODEL: WIFE OF ALCOHOLIC

Must learn to push it back in his face not take the blame--that's the old systems model and it's lame.

I'm not responsible for his drinking, he drank before he met me and it's from HIS emotional immaturity.

Wife of the Alcoholic Syndrome is one heavy debilitating disease and sad psychological malaise.

The wife of the alcoholic is his enemy when drinking and it's like living in a grenade range ALL the time.

I was responsible for marrying an immature man on that life level but at first he was all so believable.

Alcohol is a conduit to the devil and so I lived in hell and couldn't trust a thing out of his mouth.

He sided with my enemies against me, he spied on and betrayed me, he had become old and ugly.

Carol Burnett had alcoholic parents: why she's so good at portraying family pathology [like Edward Albee].

They can TELL you're not part of the group and don't wanna be--they call that "arrogance", see?

IT'S ALL GOOD

They call it "declining" years but I'd rather see it as "reclining" years--time to relax, ruminate/no tears.

Globalism: when EVERY heater of a certain brand doesn't work cuz ONE part came from a different factory.

Retirement is not the "declining years" but rather the true party of relaxation: no tears/conquered fears.

SOFT PORN, OFF COLOR JOKES, CHEESY, WEIRD

Not just porn but "soft" porn, dirty/off-color jokes, cheesy or weird things--put it all in same bag to go out.

I want a man who's not into any of that crap. No dirty jokes ever and confronting the same in others.

I want things NICE. A nice, decent, spiritual, safe and loving home which is beautiful--not your vice!

Ever seen the Golden Girls? Completely dirty, tho "classy" and degraded female culture since 1990.

This isn't the fifties--everything has changed and you even hear sex jokes from dirty old ladies.

Of course he doesn't read my work, I don't expect him to. Sit down and read 50,000 quips? I don't think so.

Town slut's favorite show: The Golden Girls. They made Blanche the slut look cute/she copied that world.

The strong have restraint, the weak do not. The problem is: surrounded by evil you just feel nuts.

WOMEN COME TO SUCCESS IN HOME

A woman comes to success in her home. In an archetypal sense, that's totally logical and I'm into it more.

IT'S ALL GOOD

I do yardwork early am hearing birds and crows. I lay in sun then resume work hearing crickets, ya' know?

This is country living, hearing these lovely sounds. The balmy wind in the aft, I'm loving my home.

This cosmic experience of nooks/crannies of home ONLY came after DELETION OF CLUTTER, all of it.

I'm into it: HOME, and it's a cosmic spiritual experience, as intense as the elements themselves I guess.

Porn: Tho' agreed it still cheats the relationship, destroyed nevertheless cuz it shrinks the brain if nothing else.

"I'll start tomorrow" made Andy really mad at Opie. In the sixties people didn't procrastinate or be lazy.

He was magnetized by her utter beauty but when she started her vicious gossiping he left immediately.

HOME IS ALL

He's irritable and short cuz he doesn't feel good. Gotta take that into account in this era of bad food.

Learning to say NO to new puppies/kittens needing homes was my biggest lesson: concern for my OWN.

Women stop acting disgraceful. Someone gives you a house and you treat it like a storage bin/garbage?

Housecats live 12-17 years, outdoor cats 2-5 years. I can understand that, I'd sure hate to be out there.

Hodgepodge: what is the ordering principal? Just a catch-all or according to type or tool?

After he was done with "neat and orderly" I spent five hours pulling more stuff out: immaturity.

IT'S ALL GOOD

Non-organic melon gave me a severe headache for two days. Never again store-bought fruit, or pay.

BIG business is open [Costco] but LITTLE businesses are not and there's NO science behind all that.

ONE meal is digestive fire in the morning. TWO means I can't focus, I'm tired, not on top of things.

I don't understand eating ONE meal at night--you wanna choke in your sleep? Happens all the time.

No, the one meal should be BREAK-FAST only. Early, then you work all day tirelessly and fast to eternity.

DINNER FOR BREAKFAST

What's for breakfast today: Roasted tomato Italian sauce over rice noodles with parmesan, ole.

Breakfast yesterday: Baked salmon/shrimp with roasted vegetables in lemon garlic butter sauce, ok!

Ray prefers to carb-up in the morning, loving the glucose rush. Blueberry muffins with butter, much.

Well I've laid it all out to you: breakfast, interest in the home, routines, fasting and utter happiness.

When it comes to cooking it must be done with empathy, thought and delicacy--can you do that Missy?

I'm energetic/elastic all day long, I think it's from carbing up in the morning then absolutely nothing.

Of course I make healthy selections but no more diet dogma--it's no one's business.

If stuffed with starch just reverse into protein and it will trigger the opposite hormones and all go out.

IT'S ALL GOOD

The sinner is a cute kid but after a few years looks worn, haggard, bloated, angry, muddy, ugly and aged.

Their concoctions look like garbage and there's too many spices. I wouldn't touch that food, yuk three times.

The idea of flavorings complementing each other delicately is lost to them, it's about quantity.

AVOID SUPERFLUITY/NON-ESSENTIALITY/DISORDERLY

From the hodgepodge of tools all around I re-ordered three tool rooms with hooks/things easily found.

He had enough tools for a warehouse, I was depressed. After weeks of ordering, I feel blessed.

It's now a well-ordered happy house not a barn, a lumber yard or a messy disarranged warehouse.

With everything else gone [old projects undone or gone wrong] I will just work the yard to stay young.

Sisters got control of finances so I couldn't buy a house with a fence around it and I was a sitting duck.

TOO MANY TOOLS AND CLOTHES

People screw you in various ways, often very subtle or indirectly thru other people while seeming humble.

His greatest legacy was all tools left to her, tho' she had no idea how to use em or even what they were.

Men have so much paraphernalia in their world ONLY a warehouse saves the marriage lest she's careless.

Never seen so much stuff in my life. I wouldn't even want a hodgepodge in storage--eliminate or make nice.

IT'S ALL GOOD

My superfluity sin: clothes. I'm relieved to have it all pared down to the best in duplicate, ya know?

IMAGE CONTROL AND CENSORSHIP

To be perfect there are **NO** tell-tall signs [TT] of what you don't wish to portray. Be thorough today.

To be logical, thorough, complex and universal in groups brands you a **TROUBLEMAKER**: get her out!

It hurts every time being banned but it always has. You're too **SMART** for em-- get that into your head.

Too deep, all-encompassing, mystical, never heard before, not part of narrative: You're **TROUBLE**.

I'm thru not being able to speak out in groups cuz I'm too deep or whatever/speaking against elite.

They act like it's finished: the arguments been made and it's **ALL-OK** but sorry buddy it's **NOT** God said.

I guess that's it for the day as duty crowds in, pets call for attention and there are things to be done.

GRACE ABUSE

We should feel remorse for sins, not abusing **GRACE** by saying "it's all ok-- forget it", being flippant.

Once rid of the old, in your new life have **HIGH CALIBRE** relationships--you interact in a certain way.

Not walking on eggshells so they won't envy, not needing to act a certain way so they will feel ok.

Sis wouldn't allow me to have an opinion different from hers, she'd always censure me at family dinners.

IT'S ALL GOOD

High caliber: Allow you having different opinions from them, respects you as an opinionated woman.

DENIAL/SEARED CONSCIENCE ARE BLOCKS

First you see the gravity of your sin--like it was a different person--then you're SO grateful to the Son.

Our lives go blank thru denial and seared conscience. SEE your shocking sin then be done with it.

Just cuz it's tucked away thru compartmentalization doesn't mean it's gone--it's an atom bomb.

I was SHOCKED to see my sin from decades back then Jesus said "it's all blacked out": that's a fact.

How could such a filthy sinner as myself be white as snow again? It was erased thru death of the Son.

I had trivialized my sin, the only way to live with it blocked within. WHEN I saw it I was instantly forgiven.

I had abused GRACE--free redemption--by being flippant knowing I was forgiven. This is arrogance.

How can you be forgiven for something you have blocked within, DENIAL of the inner trash bin?

Thinking you're great in other areas, comparing yourself to worse others--maintaining image forever.

When I saw my absurd sins the only explanation was the devil, immaturity, immorality, social hypnotism.

When I saw my sins I could not believe it then in total anguish I got on my knees and thanked Jesus.

Tears were rolling down my eyes--why did it take decades? We're all distracted by our charades.

IT'S ALL GOOD

Charades, broken trauma bonds from childhood, interlocking jealousies obsessed with Elmer Fudd.

"Oh well, forget it--I am forgiven" is not remorse--abusing grace while minimizing your filthy sins in any case.

TRUE REPENTANCE IS HUMILITY

The truly repentant never has ego problems again. He humbly knows where he's been, tho' forgiven.

Women set a new life up while ending the old--is this not survival related so we're not out in the cold?

HOW could I have ever done such a thing? The devil was in me due to weakness and social hypnotizing.

Billy Graham's tattooed grandson preaches in jeans full of holes, showing NO respect for our Father's house.

You wear your BEST to praise the Lord, not your worst or a means to attract opposite sex by brazen clothes.

Tattoos and body piercings are strictly forbidden which the bible says are ONLY worn by the heathen.

The tattooed preacher speaks ONLY of grace to cover his most recent sins not his disgrace tho' erased.

"My sins are ever before me" the bible says. It keeps us humble and releases creative action--it pays.

I'm thru with groups cuz I'm done getting hurt being misunderstood and seen as a bloody irritant.

First you're lost in a local fog, then you start to wake up, then you grow in self and awareness of God.

Since God designed True Self, insofar as you come to God you come to the blueprint of your unique spirit.

IT'S ALL GOOD

I know who I am today: talents, temperament, proclivities--because I'm humbled by the past, you see?

WE'RE ALL SINNERS

What did I do? That's not the point--we're ALL sinners, every dirty filthy lying one of us, even you.

To wake up I had to live alone in the desert wilderness for 26 years in a tiny cabin, like Abraham Lincoln.

Some famous leaders in history had to spend years in jail first. It takes what it takes to remove the curse.

Was it a generational curse? Why else would you act out the absurd, acting so atrociously and weird?

I had to get away from the subliminal cues/triggers. I was so reactive I had to find something bigger.

When she jealously looked her up and down she was relieved to see she had flabby arms: women!

Made dense by previous systems I didn't even know they disrespected me, let alone humiliated me.

Didn't even know it--had no idea. That was just the way life was I thought, middle class life in America.

The fact is I was brought up by an alcoholic brawling mother and two enemy sisters: that's it dear.

I know about women. No jilted/divorced man can tell me anything--there's nothing they won't do for revenge.

SOCIAL HYPNOTISM

They listen to their female friends who also don't know anything and it's a chicken coop happening.

IT'S ALL GOOD

My mother didn't understand my personality type bless her, she just wanted conformity to her norm sir.

Do women fear men going with their friends? Well there's much MORE to fear with hers, don't pretend.

Listen to how Blanche the Slut talks in Golden Girls: real old ladies talking dirty over cheesecake.

How many sweaters did I need? One in every color and pattern--there they sit/I never wore em, see?

I find the one shoe I can wear then buy twenty pair. This makes perfect sense since they won't be there.

Food times depends on sleep times. I bed down around 4 in the aft and arise again before midnight.

Even if I eat at noon there's a possibility of choking at night--anything in the alimentary canal ain't right.

Christians are hated for their restraint, their lines and their boundaries against evil invading their lives.

Black patent ballet flats are perfect and ladylike. All else are CLODHOPPERS and I hate em all, alright?

They're phasing out the black patent leather ballet flats for being too FEMININE. They want us manly man.

CHILDREN OF ALCOHOLICS: CAROL BURNETT

The best Carol Burnett comedies are about family pathology--she overcame it thru humor apparently.

Sibling rivalries, interlocking jealousy patterns, petty hierarchies, sterile dynasties--portrayed perfectly.

The first life was training and karma. Then when it's all paid/prepared for we enter the fruits: nirvana!

IT'S ALL GOOD

All sin has consequences, affecting looks/breaks: whether your bucket has holes or you get the sweepstakes.

Whenever I drank I'd get a bee in my bonnet that I thought was brilliant but the next day I was fired/sunk.

A bee in my bonnet: I'd get right on it like it was the greatest idea in history then: embarrassment.

Instead of dropping down into PTSD memories, say: "I went through all that/am that much stronger".

Just the fact you acted so crazy, and aren't now--shows you grew from the bad experience, ya know?

For PTSD pray God will take the thoughts away or just say: "this is what I overcame to be strong today."

I can't believe what the spiteful psychotic children did to me, I have to stop reasoning with it/let it be.

Is there any maturity left, or literacy? Is everyone dumb as a rock, herd hypnotized and blind to eternity?

Is there any woman not envious, jealously sizing females up? Is this how they're born or just f---up?

For relief from present psychosis I watch Andy in Mayberry when decency prevailed/happiness.

The crap they accused me of, from their dirty minds. They were bad but I was cast in that light.

THE DIRTY GOLDEN GIRLS

How clever: make debauched Golden Girls look cute cuz they're just innocent old ladies--genius actually.

JOB of the older women is to educate the morals of the young. but these days they just demoralize em.

IT'S ALL GOOD

Everything rests on older women cuz that's what's expected of em but men must be rock-strong.

I overcame it all, bought a new house and got the HELL out. No one to brag to, they couldn't care less.

Young men are inspired by older women opening the portals of their mind--but today she gives in.

The job of the older women is to educate the morals of the young but these days they just demoralize em.

My God I was nuts. But it helps to know it was the devil and ANYTHING can happen when he rules.

It helps to know my work stands on its own. It's not necessary that I be present/defend it, I'm gone.

I don't wanna be dominated by children anymore. They are quicksand, selfish/mean attention whores.

I took you in and you caused me so much trouble it wasn't funny. You run in groups, you're all loony.

You imposed your friends on me--flying monkeys doing your unseen dirty work while you look innocent.

Did you ever ONCE think you were invading my privacy with all your friends? A dam army of em?

I don't want anything imposed on me but with evil children it's constant when they should adapt to me.

EVIL MANIPULATIVE CHILDREN

When with evil manipulative children I'm exhausted within minutes and they can be shrewd the dickens.

They have no empathy for what you're going thru as they suck everything outa ya feeling entitled to it.

IT'S ALL GOOD

I've been under siege since 1983 when my own sister led the attack against me.

He was enamored by her beauty til she said a buncha dirty words and he was shocked & sickened.

How could I have acted like that? It was a combination of social hypnotism and being worn down.

Don't allow your youtube show to make you a slave to the same time each day: It's whenever, ok?

What if you don't feel like it, think it or don't feel inspired? Creativity can't conform to time or the hour.

Don't force it--it'll come off forced. Make your video ONLY when hot, inspired: now it's anointed.

I only write when it comes THRU not when I demand it dude. It's God and He's using each one of us.

Never, ever, ever make your God-given creativity conform to man's time schedules, you'll lose it all.

And if you must conform to a time schedule, pray and God'll pour the words in, it's predictable.

CREATIVE BY STARTING A PARTY

The way I create is by having a party. Take the day off then creative process runs without stopping.

Only by relaxing compulsive tunnel-vision do we go into the right-brain of WIDE angled vision [wisdom].

He wrote her every day for eight years even though they never met nor ever made a commitment.

Only by relaxing the tunnel-vision can we find the key which lays OUTSIDE. Start a party God said.

IT'S ALL GOOD

Jezebel left her dam boyfriend off at my house while she took a walk--without knowing if we mixed well.

I'm caught between fidelity and honor before God and what I want to do. Aren't we all? It's true.

I've climbed the highest mountain now I'm gonna live off the fruits of my labors until heaven.

It's gotta be inspired--why else would someone do all this? Are you kidding, 50 thousand quips?

People aren't that important--it's God. They come and go and as archetypes they go high or low.

SHAME AND CRITICAL PARENT

CPTSD manifests a critical inner voice tearing you down--you wake up in bad memories it's so profound.

The toxified superego is the inner parent yelling at you. I could hear inner women yelling for years too.

Child abuse by a narcissist parent manifests later in the continuous irritant of your "inner critic".

If you don't heed your parents the world will grow you up and it'll be a MUCH harsher punishment.

The narcissist psychopath always overplays his hand. If you be alert it's your chance to ban the man.

He overplayed his hand, I fought back for the first time and the cops got him for YEARS of scams.

I was so dumbed I didn't realize he always showed up on my payday, how he pressured me constantly.

EVIL MEN HYPNOTIZE WEAK WOMEN

IT'S ALL GOOD

Evil men hypnotizing weak women in their homes: always trying to get money outa me, a dam gigolo.

He had a way of physically intimidating me, by lurching forward--and I'd succumb, what a pansy.

If I didn't concede he'd come back with his friends--flying monkeys were his enforcers, me being alone.

The cops had had enough of Christopher and got a STING on him--he went to prison for a long long time.

Larry [who killed my dog] went to prison but for a meth sting and Shane was a bum loser without teeth.

God avenged me of my enemies 30 years ago thru that sting but I didn't realize it until forgiving.

It's very dangerous for a single woman to live in a small town where evil children rule, called "cool".

I was never warned about what people were like: In my parent's day things were decent and nice.

GANGS OF YOUNG MEN

Gangs of young men leaving big cities for small towns and taking over--hard to believe but it's true sir.

PTSD is lessening since replacing bad memories with His blessings like a happy home without stressing.

They are EVIL because the spirit that has made a home in them is evil--but libs won't call em evil people.

With time they're no more brash abusive kids but old toothless losers, they're not coming up here.

The reverse racism was terrible. I'd committed the terrible sin of being white, can you imagine that?

IT'S ALL GOOD

The sinner is a cute kid but after a few years looks worn, haggard, bloated, angry, muddy, ugly.

Women in power make asses of themselves by overreach if they're still basically pagan feminist witches.

Thru overreach they abuse power and lack the character it takes not to disgrace it by being sour.

They looked at me like it was my fault for starting the ball rolling when it was just the last straw reversing.

When they're young and full of themselves, looking good, the devil takes over in full blown arrogance.

Who do you think you are, taking our time up with boring stuff cuz you say you know/are the cat's meow?

SHAME REFLECTS A BROKEN BOND

Remember, all that shame you're feeling is from a broken trauma bond, what is called the Critical Parent.

After years of "fertile anarchy" inside, it all reverses into place--coming into focus with repentance.

The feminist witch will stop at nothing to get her way. The Jezebel spirit is so strong in a sadistic lady.

Whether I see them in a good/bad up/down light depends on how I see myself right now, weak or knight?

To know Self is to know your boundaries--what bugs you baby--then not letting boundary-busters in, definitely.

Because of broken bonds and traumatic attachments we seek out jerks who do the same/never finish it.

I suddenly saw what the hell I was feeling and talking about--it all made perfect sense as a matrix.

IT'S ALL GOOD

I'm a theoretician, seeing things holistically thru the right brain while thru the left you talk about nothing.

CRITICAL PARENTS AND FLYING MONKEYS

Because you were young and inexperienced you were targeted then after that, blamed for all of it.

Once they bust your boundaries it becomes a past trauma bond screaming for correction--and you love em.

Each dawn is a new beginning. Think that when your Critical Parent starts up about your sinning.

Narcissists ALWAYS use flying monkeys while they remain charming and innocent--don't ever forget that.

He brought an army in on me who stole while he remained innocent--there's no difference, see?

Maybe he didn't want to marry a woman with 8 siblings who were all-day texting/officiously involving?

Take a good look at his kids before you marry. I thought I could. change em but what a hellish memory.

Just one kid acting up destroys your life, personality and spirit. We adapt to our environment/I'd fear it.

RESTRAINT IS A STRENGTH

Restraint is a strength. It takes strength not to have a bunch of junk around: the king is restrained.

When Critical Parent starts up and you fall into bag of shame/guilt, recall EACH morn is NEW/rebuilt.

They tried to hold me back then and are doing it now thru voice inside, the Critical Parent who is snide.

IT'S ALL GOOD

I'm smarter now, I know that shame is from separation from an old system with a trauma bond.

This is what happens when mediocre people are given godlike powers. Tucker Carlson on Lockdown

When he stepped down in my view my True Self, destiny and everything I thought came through.

When I stopped being supply for the narcissist I started living this fantastic life full of rich success.

When he had his hooks in me my psyche I was drained, life seemed grey, I was unhappy/in pain.

WHEN HE HAD HIS HOOKS IN ME

I was supposed to look up to him--tho' inside I found him boring--while my own destiny faded to nothing.

It was a sting of a pit viper draining me of all energy, vitality and self-esteem: a 6-month bad dream.

Look at the past as a master pugilist: You start out getting beaten up then gradually move up to the best.

Suddenly Ray loves yard work. It's as if he's been stung and I couldn't feel more blessed, yes sir!

I was beaten up by you coming over all the time. Stalking me, wanting a part of me or to be me, oh my!

The only person I feel comfortable with is Ray who totally leaves me alone on my throne all night and day.

To think how I hankered over a discarder who gained a thrill out of making my life so much harder.

I've done it. I co-created a masterpiece, overcame my enemies, repented of tendencies, Lord I'm ready.

IT'S ALL GOOD

I started out beaten up by bullies: high resistance in the family mainly. Now I'm all muscle in divine reality.

I was beaten by bullies and all the flying monkeys in their army. 30 years with no R & R, ever: I'm ready.

Strange the only place I could get peace was in a ghost town but they invaded me there too ya' know.

I'm never bored or lonely but they're ALWAYS bored and lonely so they came to me and I wanted FREE.

WOMEN CAN'T GET PRIVACY

A woman would have to enter a convent to get privacy but then she'd have those rules and hierarchy.

The ONLY answer is a retired gentleman in the other house guarding your privacy, as I can see.

The best on the Conspiracy Against Privacy can be seen in Andy of Mayberry as people drive him crazy.

The desire to go DEEP within and explore all those inner mansions is blocked by their social expectations.

You use a lot of words to say nothing--I just don't get it and find it quite boring so goodbye, I'll be soaring.

My wonderful female mentor Jenna is building me up and breaking me free overnight it seems.

Because of a broken trauma bond in childhood I was like a fish swimming upstream sputtering and drowning.

MRS. SOCIAL CHARM IS EVIL

I never met such an evil woman yet she had the approval and love of the whole town. I hate contradiction!

IT'S ALL GOOD

So puerile and boring, so left-brained, so forced, so shallow and unentertaining-
-no thanks mate.

Making a big point about nothing so you appear hard line but it's all for attention getting, don't you see?

And then getting into so many boring points just to fill time when there's so many other things I'd like.

To know our SELF--become self-aware--the most essential is knowing our boundaries, declared.

Don't be a dam masochist by going there only to be hurt by his shit-shots making you feel low/not rare.

Now you go do YOUR thing, no more melting into HIS thing. Do you hear me darling?

ONE shit-shot making you feel low, unloved or less than and you never go there again or it's the end.

I don't know how the Great Man can stand it. He's an exemplar to us feeling persecuted night and day.

If trauma-bonded she says "I wanna have his baby" as she's swept up. Don't do this, prance your stuff.

You act like you're saying something when you're not saying anything and I'm done darling.

He does pointless interviews with shallow but popular people and it shows his own thoughts are low.

These disparate quips come together later in your mind: little releasors of old anchors from the past or the gutter.

100 KAREN KELLOCK BOOKS

AFFINITY OR MISERY
AGELESS CORNUCOPIA
AMERICA AWAKE!
AMERICA'S DAFT ERA
ARTS OF PALEO FASTING
AUTOPHAGY ON CHEATERS
BACKSTABBING NEUROTICS
BETRAYAL TRAUMA
BOOMERS AND BROKENNESS
BOOT ON NECK
CHAMPION GUIDES
COMMIE NUTHOUSE
COMMIES
COMMUNIST SPIRIT
CONTAGION OF MADNESS
CONTAGIOUS MADNESS
CULTURE CLASH BASHED
DAFT LEFT
DAILY FASTARIAN
DAM RATS
DIVERSITY IS CRUELTY
E-RACE WHITE
EVIL FREAKS (Beyond Gross)
THE END OR A BEND?
FEMALE BULLIES AND FEMI-NAZIS
FEMALE CARNALITY
FEMALE DUMB DOWN
FEMALE POWER DRIVE
FEMINISM AND RUIN 1 & 2
FIX FOR MISFITS
FOOLS & TRAMPS
FREEDOM SPEAKING
FRENEMY ENABLER
FRENEMY LIAR
FRENEMY THIEF
FRENEMY TRAITOR
TRENEMY TYRANT
GENIUS IS HELD DOWN
GLOBALISLAM
GOD USES THE FLAWED
HAZE OF THE LATTER DAYS

AUTHOR BIO

Karen Kellock Ph.D.

Ph.D Political Psychology, UCI 1976
Post-Doctoral: UCI Medical School
Department of Psychiatry
Grants NIMH, NIAAA

Ph.D. dissertation "A Systems-Theoretic View of Pathologic Interaction" made an early mark as the "Wife of the Alcoholic Syndrome". Postdoctoral research at UCI Medical, Dept. of Psychiatry on the systems surrounding pathology on NIMH and NIAAA federal grants: *The Contagion of Madness: The Psychology of Neurotic Interaction and Pathological Systems*. Therapy tool Therapeutic Playwriting introduced the play *Mary and Murv: Gruesome Twosomes in the Alcoholic Marriage*. She taught Abnormal Psychology and Pathological Systems Theory at UC and CSU campuses and developed "the Debris Theory of Disease" in five books and website: (www.karenkellock.org): *Champion Guides, Daily Fastarian, Just Skip Dinner, Arts of Paleo Fasting, Ageless Cornucopia. Manual for Superior Men is a* pick-it-up-anywhere book that you can't put down (20,000 Kellockialisms) and ever on your desktop it should be found (or this Ebook for superior wordsearch of new jargon).